漢字遊戲

Early Start Chinese

第一冊
Workbook 1

1

Anchia Tai · Gary Chung

自序

我是一位在美國的自學媽媽，孩子的中文學習完全由我親自教導。

在傳統教學方式的薰陶下許多家長認為孩子學中文必須先從注音開始，往往也認為中文字筆畫眾多複雜對小孩來說太難。其實對幼兒來說每一個中文字都只是一個圖案，幼兒的記憶力非常強，認字對他們來說並不困難。

我自己的兩個孩子都是從認字開始學習中文的。當初我會設計漢字遊戲是因為在市面上並沒有找到令我完全滿意的教材，絕大多數的教材都是從注音符號或是筆畫簡單的字開始教學。雖然筆劃較少容易書寫但往往這些字在日常生活上並不常見，在孩子的世界裡更是沒有應用的機會。而市面上認字的教材卻普遍地缺乏動手的參與感。孩子在學習的過程中常常覺得教材枯燥乏味，既沒趣味又缺乏實用性。這樣的學習對孩子來說不但痛苦也沒有效率。使用這些教材後我發現自己一直在動手製作輔助教材來提昇孩子的學習興趣。

我一直深信一定要讓孩子覺得有趣和實用，他們才會有學習的動力，有了動力才會學得好。所以漢字遊戲的設計是以先教常用字的方式讓孩子能夠快速進入閱讀，因而發覺識字的實用性。當孩子懂得如何應用文字後，學習自信自然就提高了。製作輔助教材時為了幫助孩子加強對生字的記憶，除了使用字卡和遊戲的方式複習，我也設計了一系列的遊戲習題，而這些習題就是漢字遊戲的誕生。

最後非常感謝您選擇漢字遊戲做為孩子的教材，也希望這套教材可以幫助您的孩子快樂學習中文。

Preface

I am a homeschooling mom in America who successfully taught my two children to read Chinese at a young age.

Many people think that learning Chinese must start with pinyin because Chinese characters are too complicated and believed to be too difficult for children. However, in a children's mind, each Chinese character is just like a picture and memorization is not difficult for them.

Both my children learned to read Chinese beginning with character recognition, yet the process was not easy for me. Existing textbooks often start teaching with pinyin or start with rarely used characters with minimal strokes for writing. Books that emphasize character recognition also tend to be less interactive and less hands-on causing the learning process to be tedious and unmotivating for children. I found myself constantly needing to create my own teaching materials while using these textbooks; and this is the reason for the creation of Early Start Chinese.

Early Start Chinese is designed to teach the most commonly used Chinese characters first, quickly allowing children to be able to read meaningful phrases and sentences from the very beginning. Pictures and games are also used to help with character retention, and each lesson includes reading passages to review previously learned characters.

Today, I am sharing with you this wonderful system that I have used with my own children and hoping to make your child's Chinese learning an easy and enjoyable journey.

每當完成一課後請回到本頁將該課的星星塗上顏色。
Please color a star after you have completed a lesson.

Lesson 1 Wǒ – I; me

在畫框內貼上或畫上自己的圖並唸出畫框下的文字。
Paste or draw your self-portrait and read aloud the character at the bottom.

找出「我」字圈出來。

Find the characters 我 and circle them.

我　　　　戈

　　我　　我

我

手　　的

　你　我

唸唸看
Read-Aloud

我
I; me

恭喜你完成了這一課，請回到第三頁將本課的星星塗上顏色。

Congratulations! You have completed a lesson. Please color the star for this lesson on page 3.

Lesson 2 De – possessive particle

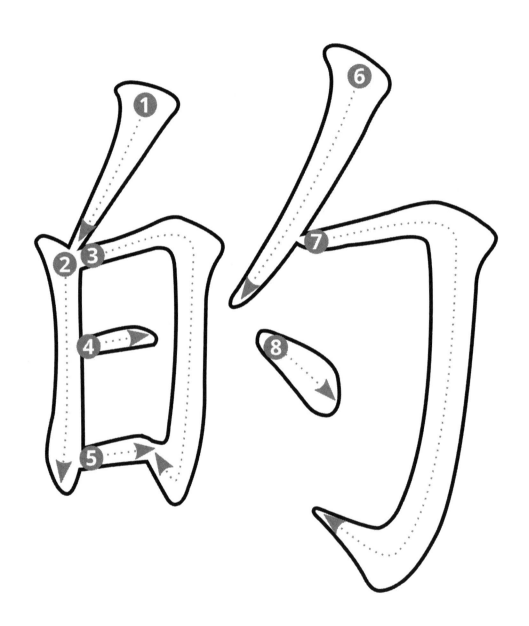

在藏寶箱內畫上自己的寶貝並唸出下方的文字。

Draw your treasure in the treasure chest and read aloud the characters at the bottom.

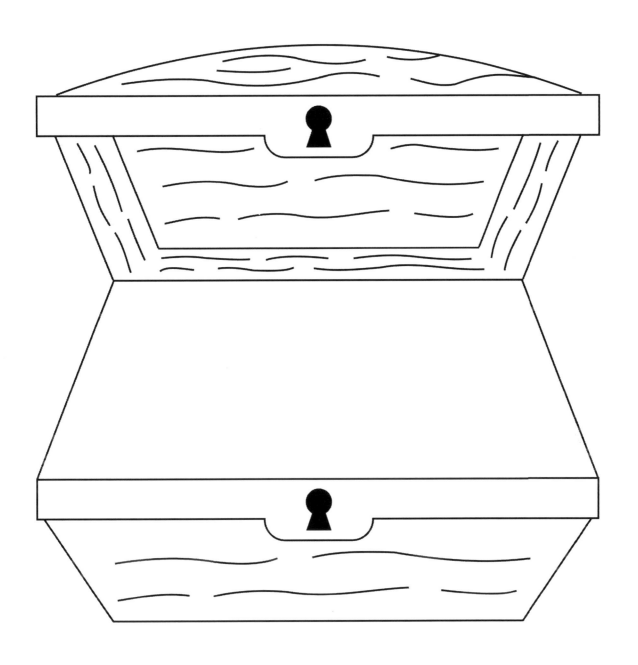

我的

跟著「的」字走幫小狗找到骨頭。

Follow the character 的 to help the puppy find the bone.

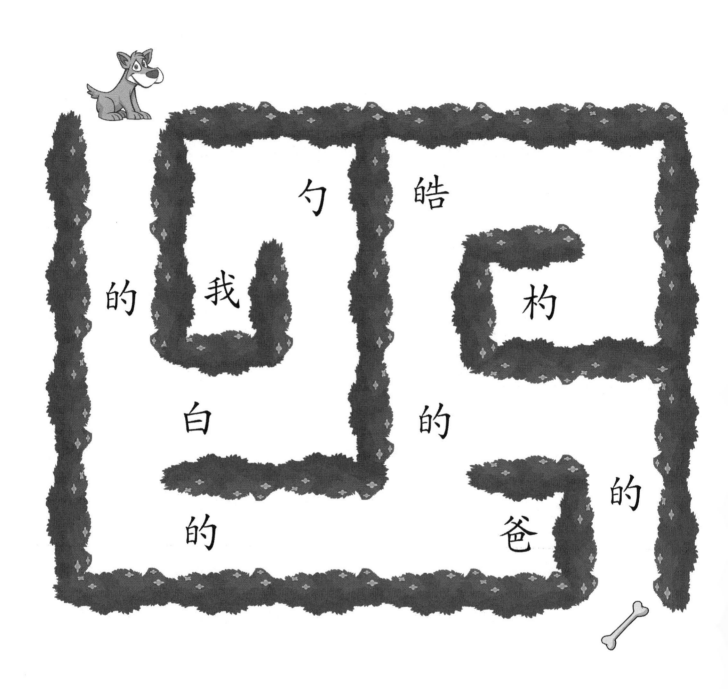

唸唸看
Read-Aloud

● 我的

My; mine

恭喜你完成了這一課，請回到第三頁將本課的星星塗上顏色。

Congratulations! You have completed a lesson. Please color the star for this lesson on page 3.

Lesson 3 Mā – mother; mom

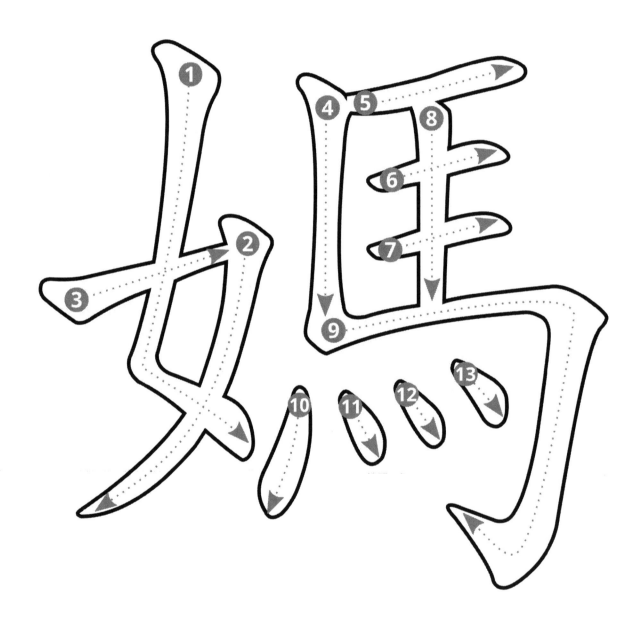

在畫框內貼上或畫上媽媽的圖並唸出畫框下的文字。

Paste or draw a picture of your mother and read aloud the characters at the bottom.

我 的 媽 媽

請將下方的字格剪下來讓孩子選擇正確的字貼上。

Please cut out the characters at the bottom and paste the correct one.

女 + 馬 = 媽

女 馬 媽 我 的

唸唸看
Read-Aloud

- 我
  I; me

- 我的
  My; mine

- 媽媽
  Mom

- 媽媽的
  Mom's

- 我的媽媽
  My mom

恭喜你完成了這一課，請回到第三頁將本課的星星塗上顏色。

Congratulations! You have completed a lesson. Please color the star for this lesson on page 3.

第四課

Lesson 4 Bà – father; dad

在畫框內貼上或畫上爸爸的圖並唸出畫框下的文字。
Paste or draw a picture of your father and read aloud the characters at the bottom.

我的爸爸

連連看。
Connect the pictures to the correct words.

•   •爸爸

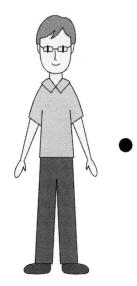

•   •媽媽

•   •我

唸唸看
Read-Aloud

- # 我的爸爸
  My dad

- # 我的媽媽
  My mom

- # 爸爸媽媽的
  Dad and mom's

- # 爸爸的
  Dad's

恭喜你完成了這一課，請回到第三頁將本課的星星塗上顏色。

Congratulations! You have completed a lesson. Please color the star for this lesson on page 3.

第五課

Lesson 5 Ài – love

連連看一樣的字。
Draw a line to the matching character.

22

將下方的字格剪下來讓孩子貼在喜愛的人和物旁。
Cut out the character blocks below and paste them next to the people and items you love.

唸唸看
Read-Aloud

- # 爸爸愛我。
  Dad loves me.

- # 媽媽愛我。
  Mom loves me.

- # 我愛我的爸爸。
  I love my dad.

- # 我愛我的媽媽。
  I love my mom.

- # 我愛爸爸媽媽。
  I love Dad and Mom.

恭喜你完成了這一課，請回到第三頁將本課的星星塗上顏色。

Congratulations! You have completed a lesson. Please color the star for this lesson on page 3.

第六課

Lesson 6 Yě – also

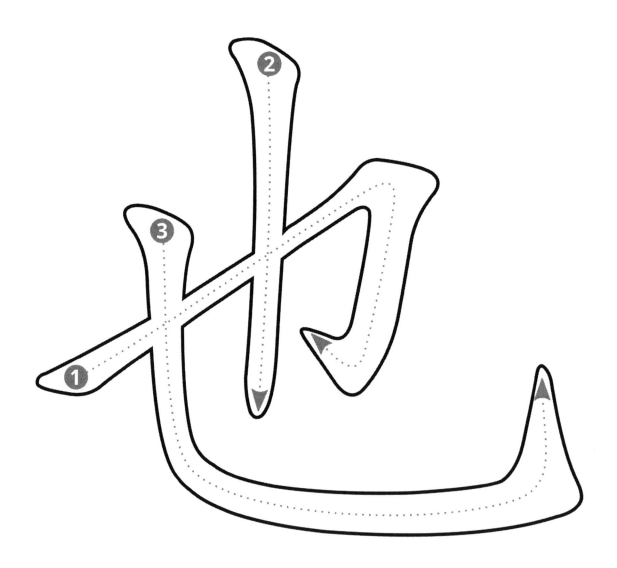

請將有「也」字的地方著色。

Color the areas with the character 也.

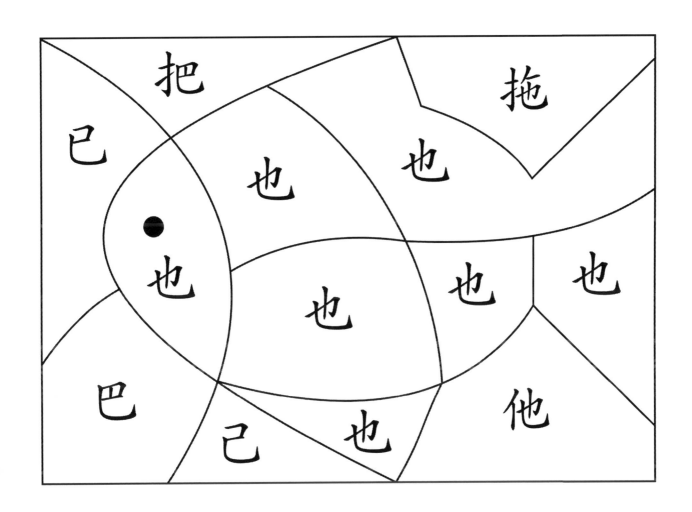

跟著「也」字從 到 ★ 走出迷宮。

Follow the character 也 from the arrow to the star to exit the maze.

也	巴	我	的	的
也	爸	媽	巴	好
也	他	也	也	也
也	也	也	媽	也
把	愛	的	爸	也

唸唸看
Read-Aloud

- # 我愛爸爸。
  I love Dad.

- # 爸爸也愛我。
  Dad also loves me.

- # 我愛媽媽。
  I love Mom.

- # 媽媽也愛我。
  Mom also loves me.

- # 我愛我的爸媽。
  I love my Dad and Mom.

恭喜你完成了這一課，請回到第三頁將本課的星星塗上顏色。

Congratulations! You have completed a lesson. Please color the star for this lesson on page 3.

第七課

Lesson 7 Yào – want; get

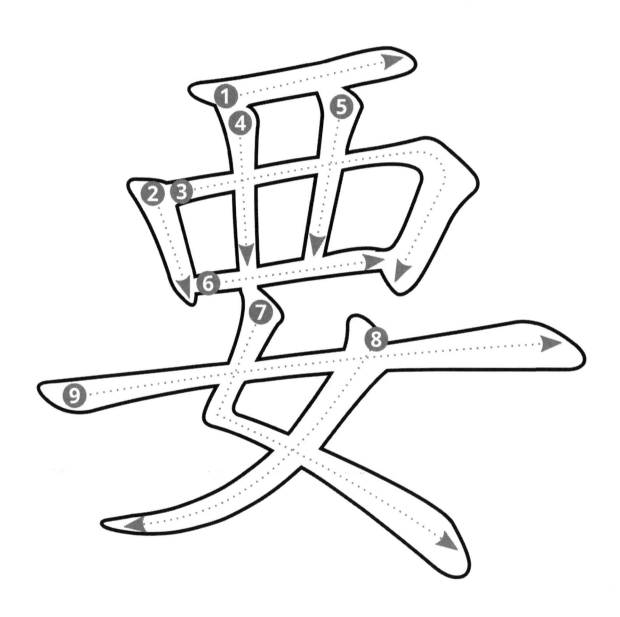

找出「要」字圈出來。

Find the characters 要 and circle them.

要　爸　西

女　要

的　要

要　媽

要　我

30

跟著「要」字走幫小企鵝找到魚。
Follow the character 要 to help the penguin find the fish.

唸唸看
Read-Aloud

- 我要媽媽的

  I want Mom's

- 我也要爸爸的

  I also want Dad's

- 我愛媽媽。

  I love Mom.

- 媽媽也愛我。

  Mom also loves me.

- 我要爸爸媽媽。

  I want Dad and Mom.

恭喜你完成了這一課，請回到第三頁將本課的星星塗上顏色。

Congratulations! You have completed a lesson. Please color the star for this lesson on page 3.

Lesson 8 Bù – no; don't

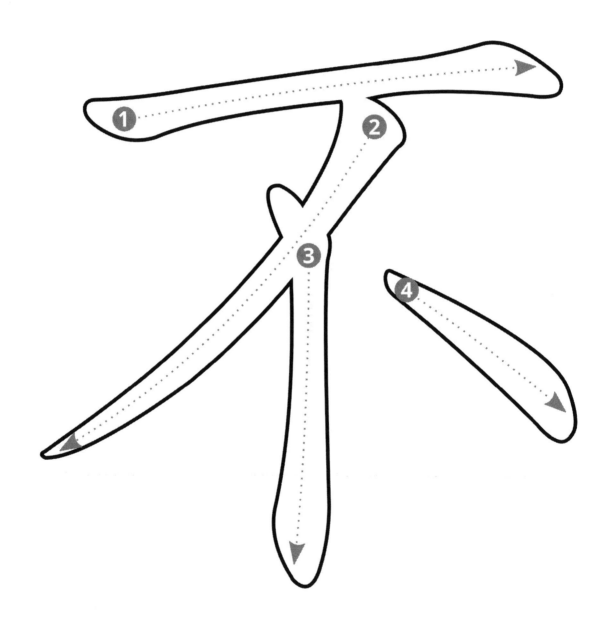

連連看一樣的字。
Draw a line to the matching character.

在不可以做的事旁貼上「不」字。

Paste the character 不 next to things you shouldn't do.

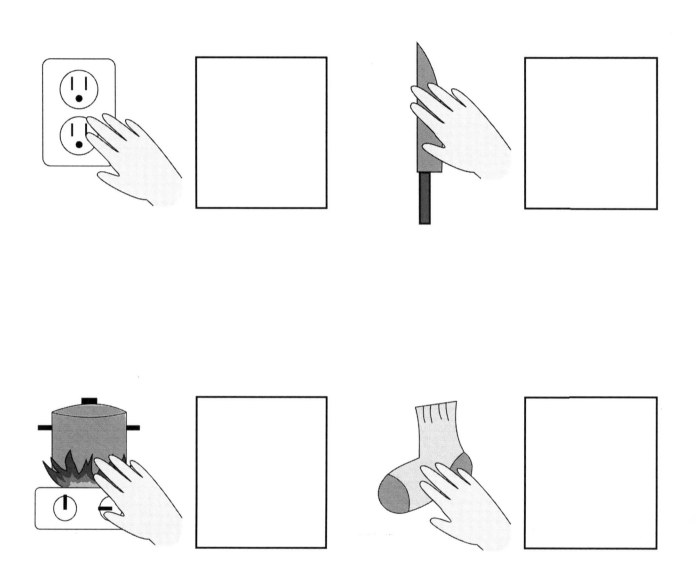

唸唸看
Read-Aloud

- 媽媽要的我也要。
  What Mom wants, I also want.

- 媽媽不要的，我也不要。
  What Mom doesn't want, I also don't want.

- 爸爸愛的，我也愛。
  What Dad loves, I also love.

恭喜你完成了這一課，請回到第三頁將本課的星星塗上顏色。

Congratulations! You have completed a lesson. Please color the star for this lesson on page 3.

Lesson 9 Jiā – home

小狗要走哪條路才可以回到家？
Which path will take the puppy home?

請將下方的字格剪下來選擇正確的字貼上。

Please cut out the characters at the bottom and paste the correct ones.

我愛我的 家 。

爸爸也愛 家 。

媽媽也愛 家 。

家 愛 家 媽 家

唸唸看
Read-Aloud

- 我愛我的家。

  I love my home.

- 我也愛爸爸媽媽。

  I also love Dad and Mom.

- 爸媽不要的，我也不要。

  What Dad and Mom don't want, I also don't want.

恭喜你完成了這一課，請回到第三頁將本課的星星塗上顏色。

Congratulations! You have completed a lesson. Please color the star for this lesson on page 3.

第十課

Lesson 10 Zài – at

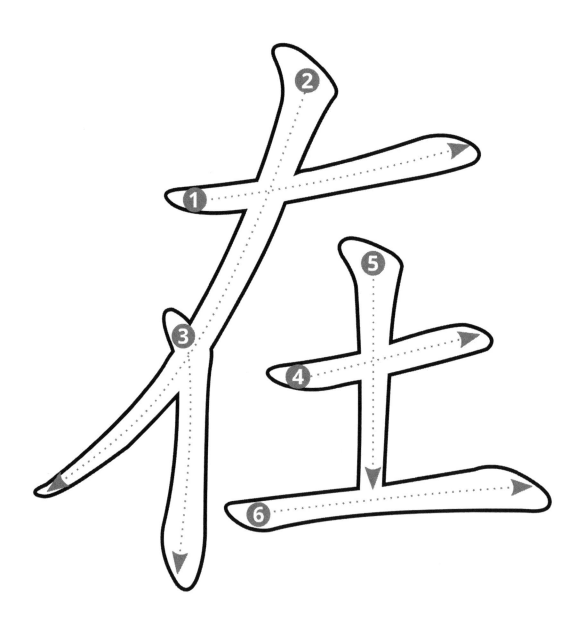

跟著「在」字從 到 ★ 走出迷宮。

Follow the character 在 from the arrow to the star to exit the maze.

在	在	在	的	媽
個	爸	在	有	也
也	我	在	要	不
也	家	在	在	在
很	愛	的	爸	在

找出「在」字圈出來。

Find the characters 在 and circle them.

在 　　　　存

土 　個 　在

在 　很 　王

　　　　　在

唸唸看
Read-Aloud

- 我在家。
  I'm at home.

- 爸爸也在家。
  Dad's also at home.

- 媽媽不在家。
  Mom's not at home.

- 我要我的媽媽。
  I want my mom.

- 媽媽愛我。
  Mom loves me.

恭喜你完成了這一課，請回到第三頁將本課的星星塗上顏色。

Congratulations! You have completed a lesson. Please color the star for this lesson on page 3.

第十一課

Lesson 11 Hěn – very

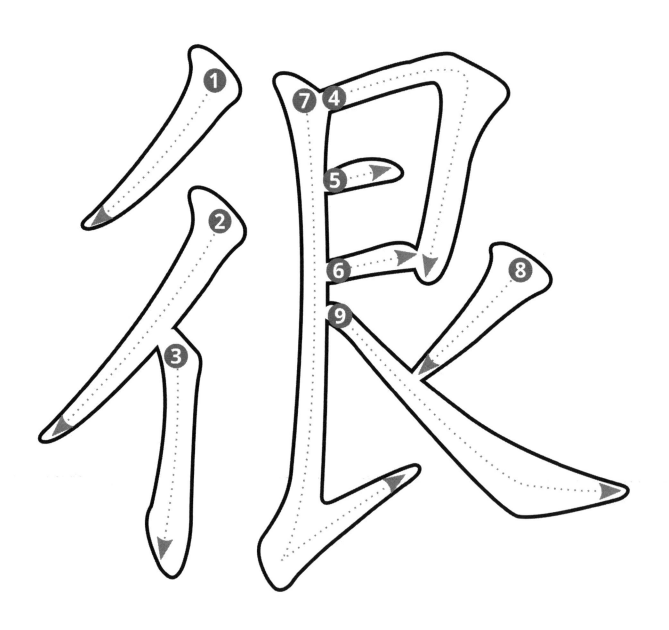

跟著「很」字走幫兔子找到紅蘿蔔。
Follow the character 很 to help the bunny find the carrot.

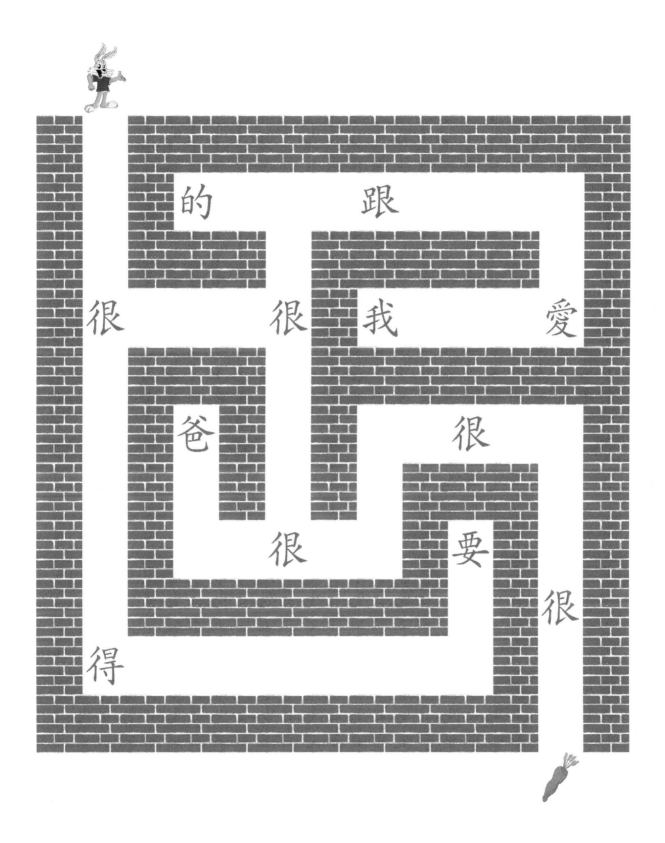

連連看一樣的字。
Draw a line to the matching character.

連連看一樣的字。
Draw a line to the matching character.

唸唸看
Read-Aloud

- 我很愛媽媽。
  I love Mom very much.

- 也很愛爸爸。
  (I) also love Dad very much.

- 我很愛我的家。
  I love my home very much.

- 我不在家。
  I'm not at home.

- 我要在家。
  I want to be at home.

恭喜你完成了這一課，請回到第三頁將本課的星星塗上顏色。

Congratulations! You have completed a lesson. Please color the star for this lesson on page 3.

第十二課

Lesson 12 Dà – big

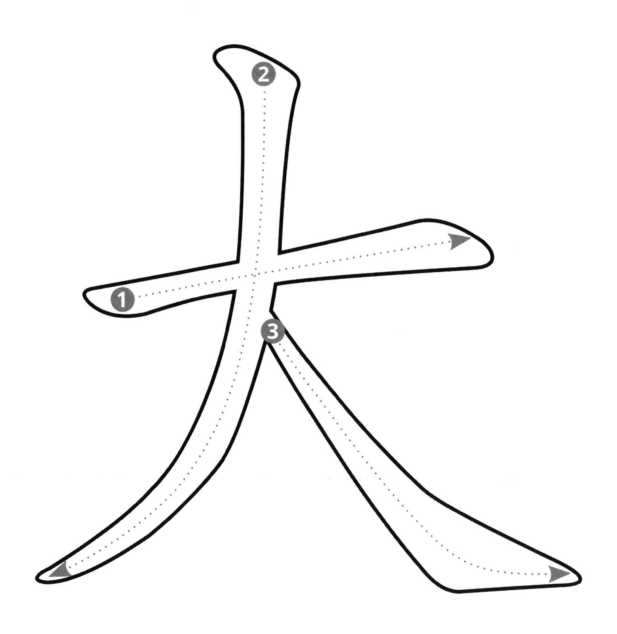

做出「大」字的動作加強對此字的記憶。

Use your body to mimic the character 大.

請將有「大」字的地方著色。

Color the areas with the character 大.

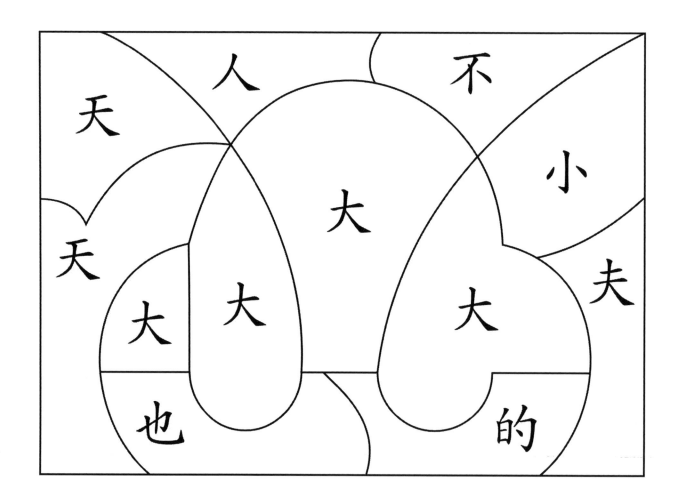

唸唸看
Read-Aloud

- 我的爸爸很大。

  My dad is very big.

- 我的媽媽也很大。

  My mom is also very big.

- 我的家也很大。

  My home is also very big.

- 我愛在我的家。

  I love to be at my home.

恭喜你完成了這一課，請回到第三頁將本課的星星塗上顏色。

Congratulations! You have completed a lesson. Please color the star for this lesson on page 3.

第十三課

Lesson 13 Xiǎo – small

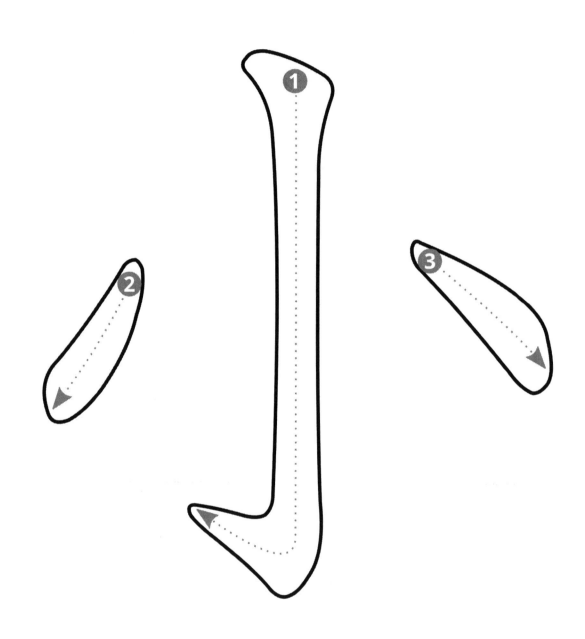

做出「小」字的動作加強對此字的記憶。
Use your body to mimic the character 小.

連連看。
Connect the pictures to the correct words.

大

小

連連看。
Connect the pictures to the correct words.

唸唸看
Read-Aloud

- 爸爸很大。
  Dad is very big.

- 我很小。
  I am very small.

- 我的家很小。
  My home is very small.

- 我愛小的家。
  I love small homes.

- 不愛很大的家。
  (I) don't love very big homes.

恭喜你完成了這一課，請回到第三頁將本課的星星塗上顏色。

Congratulations! You have completed a lesson. Please color the star for this lesson on page 3.

第十四課

Lesson 14 Shì – is

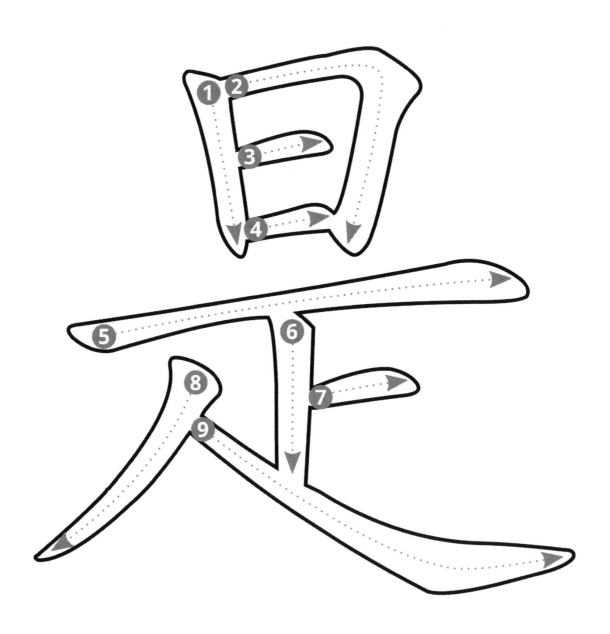

將「是」字塗色，幫小貓找到回家的路。
Color the characters 是 to find the path home.

找出「是」字圈出來。

Find the characters 是 and circle them.

是　　　走

　　旦　　　是

雲　　是

　　　　來

　　是　　　的

唸唸看
Read-Aloud

- 媽媽是愛我的。
Mom does love me.

- 爸爸也是。
Dad also does.

- 我是爸爸媽媽的。
I am Dad and Mom's.

- 我的家是很大的。
My home is very big.

- 我要在家。
I want to be at home.

恭喜你完成了這一課，請回到第三頁將本課的星星塗上顏色。

Congratulations! You have completed a lesson. Please color the star for this lesson on page 3.

第十五課

Lesson 15 Rén – person; man

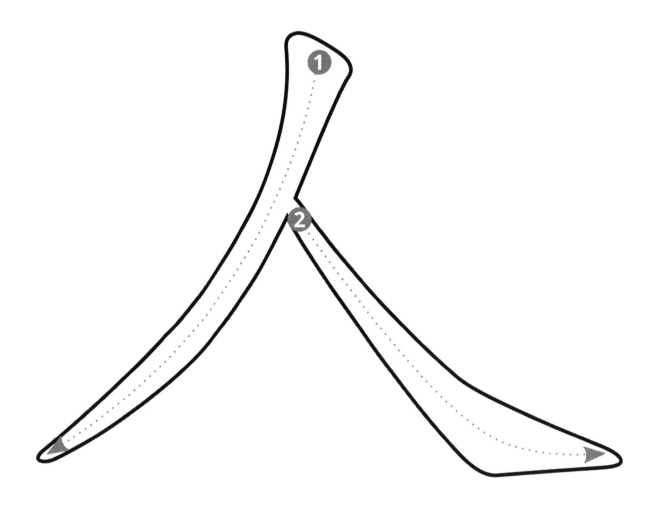

做出「人」字的動作加強對此字的記憶。

Use your body to mimic the character 人.

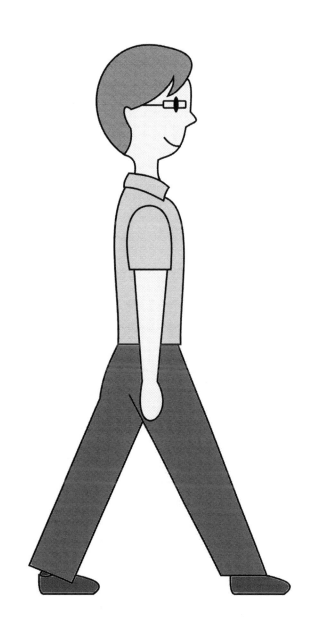

做出「人」字的動作加強對此字的記憶。

Use your body to mimic the character 人.

連連看。

Connect the pictures to the correct words.

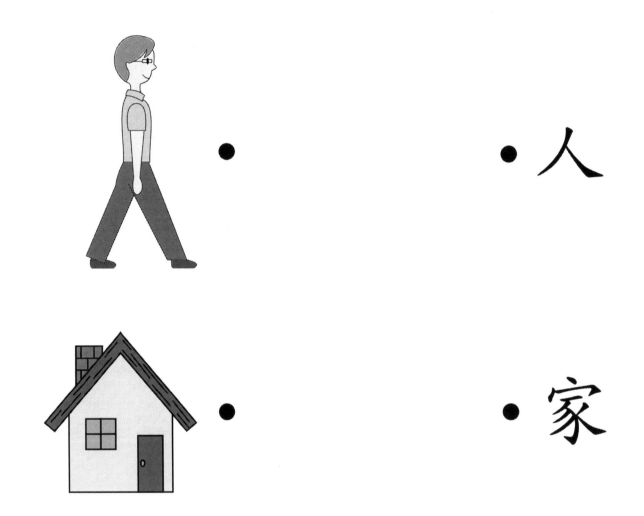

人

家

唸唸看
Read-Aloud

- 爸爸是大人。

  Dad is an adult.

- 媽媽也是大人。

  Mom also is an adult.

- 我不是大人。

  I am not an adult.

- 大人很大。

  Adults are very big.

- 我很小。

  I am very small.

恭喜你完成了這一課，請回到第三頁將本課的星星塗上顏色。

Congratulations! You have completed a lesson. Please color the star for this lesson on page 3.

第十六課

Lesson 16 Māo – cat

請將下方的字格剪下來讓孩子選擇正確的字貼上。

Please cut out the characters at the bottom and paste the correct one.

豸 + 苗 = 貓

貓　苗　豸　豬　狗

跟著「貓」字走幫小貓找到魚。

Follow the character 貓 to help the cat find the fish.

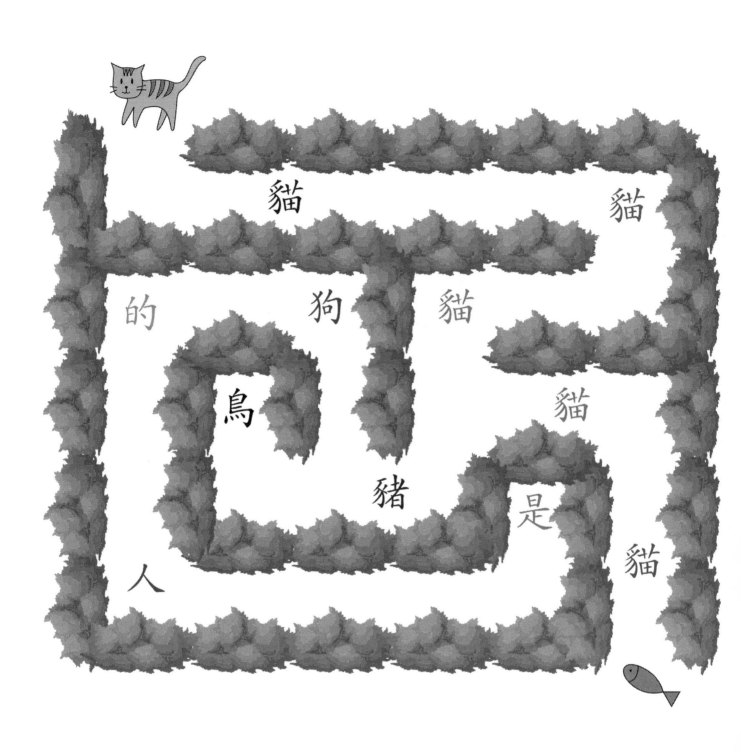

唸唸看
Read-Aloud

- 我的貓很小。

  My cat is very small.

- 小貓不愛在家。

  Little cat does not love to be at home.

- 爸爸是人。

  Dad is a person.

- 爸爸不是貓。

  Dad is not a cat.

- 爸爸在家。

  Dad is at home.

恭喜你完成了這一課，請回到第三頁將本課的星星塗上顏色。

Congratulations! You have completed a lesson. Please color the star for this lesson on page 3.

第十七課

Lesson 17 Zhī – a measure word, for some animals and more

連連看一樣的字。
Draw a line to the matching character.

請將有「隻」字的地方著色。
Color the areas with the character 隻.

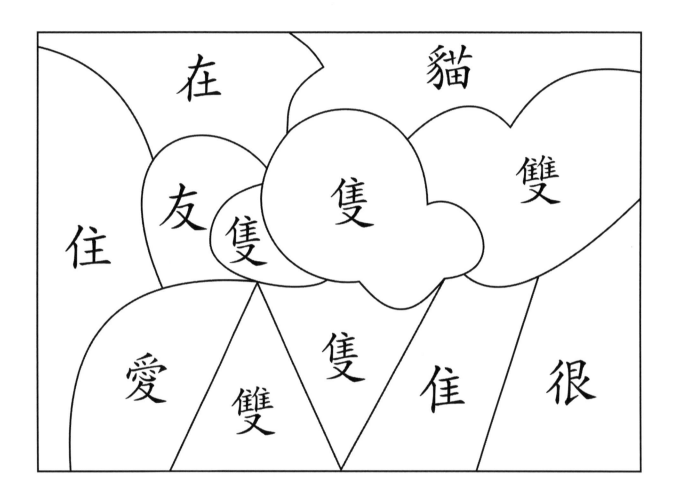

請將有「隻」字的地方著色。
Color the areas with the character 隻.

唸唸看
Read-Aloud

- 我的貓是隻小貓。

My cat is a small cat.

- 不是隻大貓。

(It is) not a big cat.

- 小貓很愛媽媽。

Little cat loves Mom very much.

- 我也很愛媽媽。

I also love Mom very much.

恭喜你完成了這一課，請回到第三頁將本課的星星塗上顏色。

Congratulations! You have completed a lesson. Please color the star for this lesson on page 3.

第十八課

Lesson 18 Yī – one

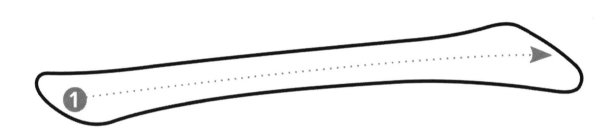

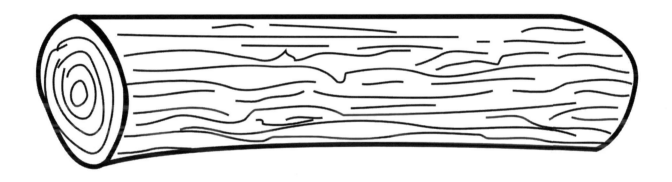

「一」字是象形字，就像根橫置的木柴。請將木柴著色。

The character for one is a pictograph depicted by a wooden stick. Please color the picture below.

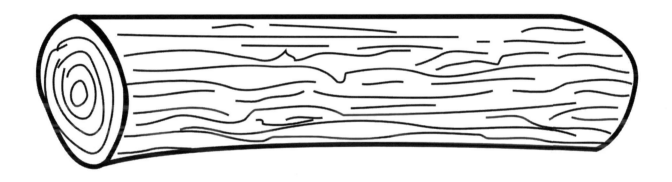

找出「一」字圈出來。

Find the characters 一 and circle them.

唸唸看
Read-Aloud

- 一隻貓是大貓。

  One cat is a big cat.

- 一隻貓是小貓。

  One cat is a small cat.

- 媽媽要一隻小貓。

  Mom wants one small cat.

- 不要一隻大貓。

  (She) does not want a big cat.

- 我也愛小的貓。

  I also love small cats.

恭喜你完成了這一課，請回到第三頁將本課的星星塗上顏色。

Congratulations! You have completed a lesson. Please color the star for this lesson on page 3.

第十九課

Lesson 19 Huā – flower

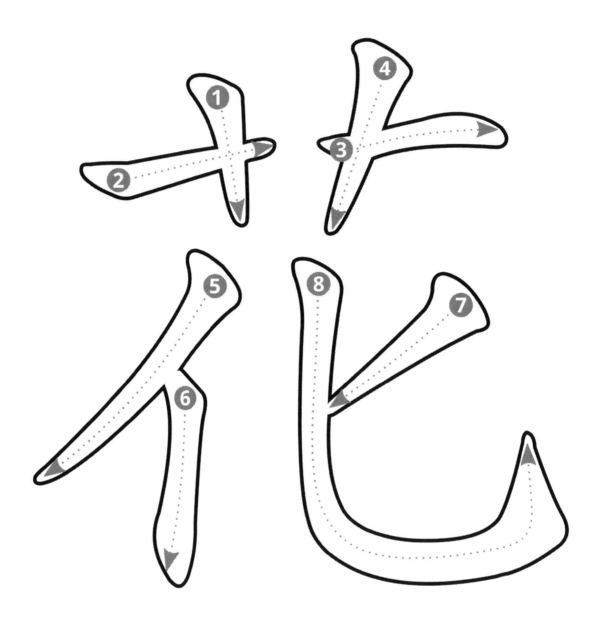

畫上美麗的花朵並唸出下方的文字。

Draw beautiful flowers and read aloud the character at the bottom.

花

連連看。
Connect the pictures to the correct words.

 · · 花

 · · 貓

 · · 我

唸唸看
Read-Aloud

● 一隻小花貓在家。

One small multicolored cat is at home.

● 媽媽愛花。

Mom loves flowers.

● 我也愛花。

I also love flowers.

● 爸爸是大人。

Dad is an adult.

● 大人很大。

Adults are very big.

恭喜你完成了這一課，請回到第三頁將本課的星星塗上顏色。

Congratulations! You have completed a lesson. Please color the star for this lesson on page 3.

第二十課

Lesson 20 Niǎo – bird

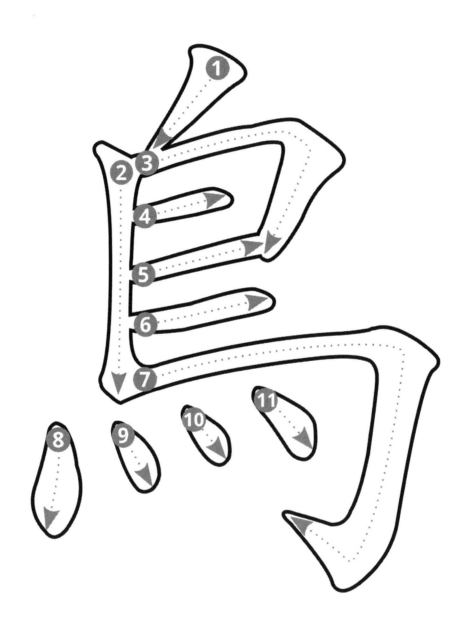

「鳥」字是象形字，就像鳥頭上的羽毛、眼睛、翅膀、尾巴和爪子等部分被畫出來一樣。請將小鳥著色。

The character for bird is a pictograph, the feather on top of the head, eye, wing, tail and claws forms the character. Please color the picture below.

圖案中有的東西在（　）中打勾。

Put a check next to the items that are in the picture.

（　）家　　（　）貓　　（　）鳥

（　）花　　（　）人

唸唸看
Read-Aloud

- # 一隻小鳥
  One small bird

- # 小貓不愛花。
  Little cat does not love flowers.

- # 小貓很愛小鳥。
  Little cat loves little bird very much.

- # 小鳥不愛小貓。
  Little bird does not love little cat.

- # 小鳥愛人。
  Little bird loves people.

恭喜你完成了這一課，請回到第三頁將本課的星星塗上顏色。

Congratulations! You have completed a lesson. Please color the star for this lesson on page 3.

第二十一課

Lesson 21 Yǒu – have

跟著「有」字走幫女孩摘到星星。

Follow the character 有 to help the girl reach the stars.

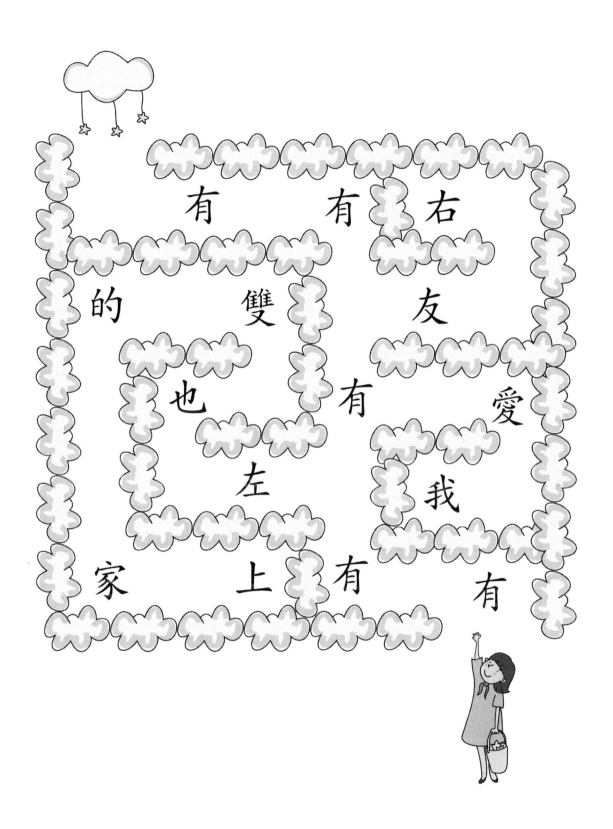

連連看一樣的字。

Draw a line to the matching character.

唸唸看
Read-Aloud

- 我家有花。
There are flowers at my home.

- 我家也有鳥。
There are also birds at my home.

- 我有一隻小花貓。
I have a small multicolored cat.

- 我有爸爸媽媽。
I have Dad and Mom.

- 爸媽是愛我的人。
Dad and Mom are people who loves me.

恭喜你完成了這一課，請回到第三頁將本課的星星塗上顏色。

Congratulations! You have completed a lesson. Please color the star for this lesson on page 3.

第二十二課

Lesson 22 Méi – not

請將有「沒」字的地方著色。

Color the areas with the character 沒.

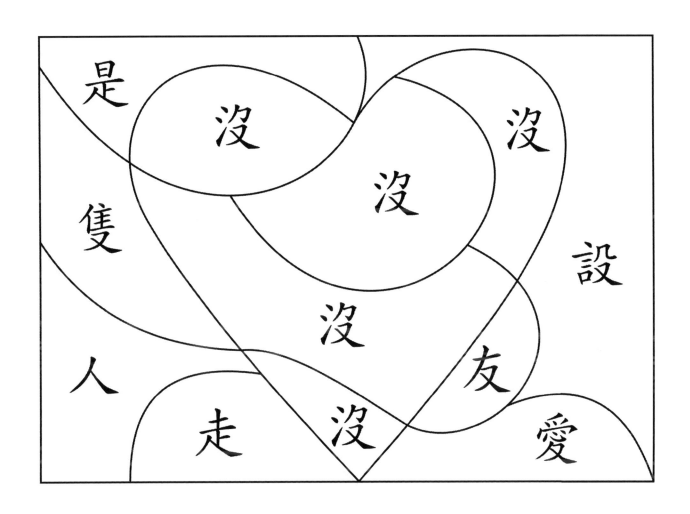

將「沒」字塗色，幫小蜜蜂找到回家的路。
Color the characters 沒 to find the path home.

		沒			
隻	又	沒			
要		沒	沒	沒	沒
人	日	上			沒
在		去	走	是	沒
大	不	爸			沒

將「沒」字塗色，幫小蜜蜂找到回家的路。
Color the characters 沒 to find the path home.

唸唸看
Read-Aloud

- # 我沒有一隻大貓。
  I do not have a big cat.

- # 也沒有大鳥。
  (I) also do not have big birds.

- # 我家有很大的花。
  There is a very big flower in my home.

- # 小貓不要花。
  Little cat does not want flowers.

- # 小貓愛小鳥。
  Little cat loves little bird.

恭喜你完成了這一課，請回到第三頁將本課的星星塗上顏色。

Congratulations! You have completed a lesson. Please color the star for this lesson on page 3.

第二十三課

Lesson 23 Tóu – head

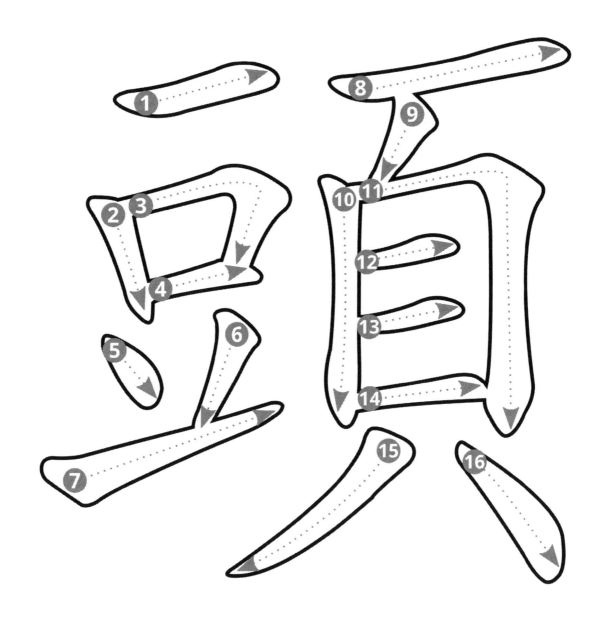

連連看。
Connect the pictures to the correct words.

 •

• 花

 •

• 頭

 •

• 鳥

找出「頭」字圈出來。

Find the characters 頭 and circle them.

頭　　　豆

頁　個　頭

頭　　家

頭　　的

唸唸看
Read-Aloud

- 爸爸的頭很大。

Dad's head is very big.

- 我也有很大的頭。

I also have a very big head.

- 小鳥的頭很小。

Little bird's head is very small.

- 花有沒有頭？

Do flowers have heads?

- 家有沒有頭？

Do homes have heads?

恭喜你完成了這一課，請回到第三頁將本課的星星塗上顏色。

Congratulations! You have completed a lesson. Please color the star for this lesson on page 3.

第二十四課

Lesson 24 Shàng – up; on top

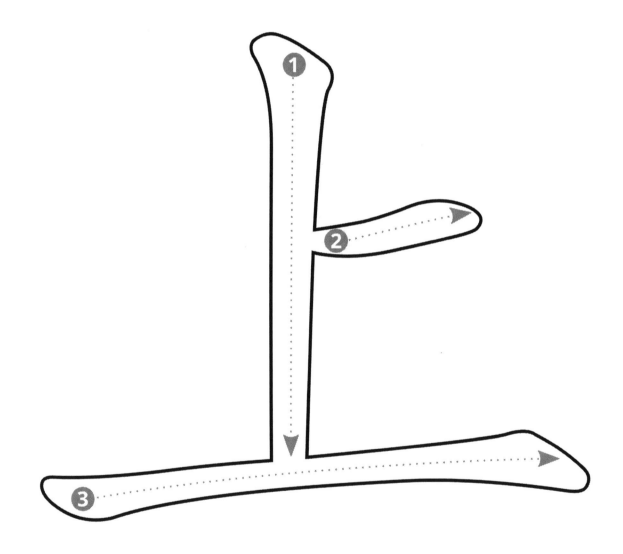

「上」字就像是地上站著一個人手指著上方。
The character 上 is like a person standing on flat floor pointing upward.

「上」字就像是地上站著一個人手指著上方。
The character 上 is like a person standing on flat floor pointing upward.

請將下方的字格剪下來選擇正確的字貼上。
Please cut out the characters at the bottom and paste the correct ones.

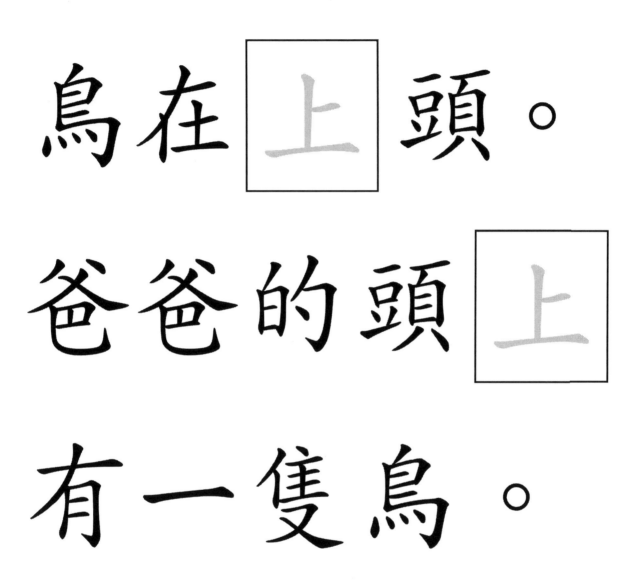

鳥在 上 頭。

爸爸的頭 上

有一隻鳥。

上　上　不　上　下

唸唸看
Read-Aloud

- # 小鳥的頭上有花。
  There is a flower on little bird's head.

- # 貓的頭上有小鳥。
  There is a little bird on top of cat's head.

- # 有一隻貓在我頭上。
  There is a cat on top of my head.

- # 我在爸爸的頭上。
  I am on top of Dad's head.

- # 爸爸的頭很大。
  Dad's head is very big.

恭喜你完成了這一課，請回到第三頁將本課的星星塗上顏色。

Congratulations! You have completed a lesson. Please color the star for this lesson on page 3.

第二十五課

Lesson 25 Gè – a measure word

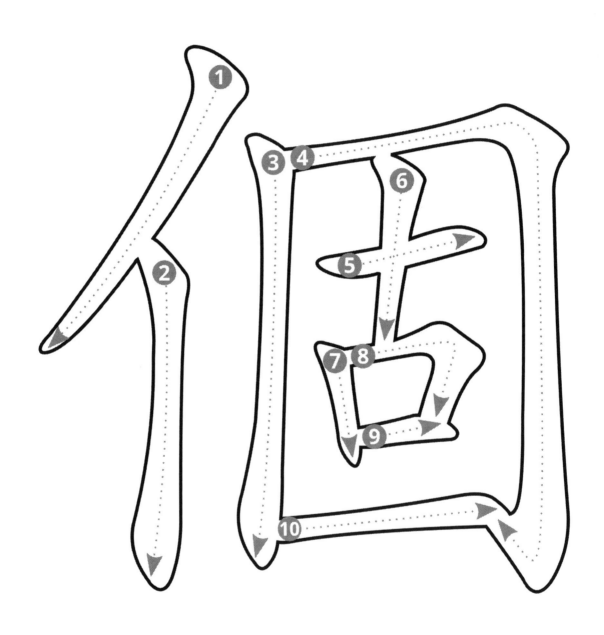

跟著「個」字走把拖拉機開回農舍。

Follow the character 個 to drive the tractor back to the barn.

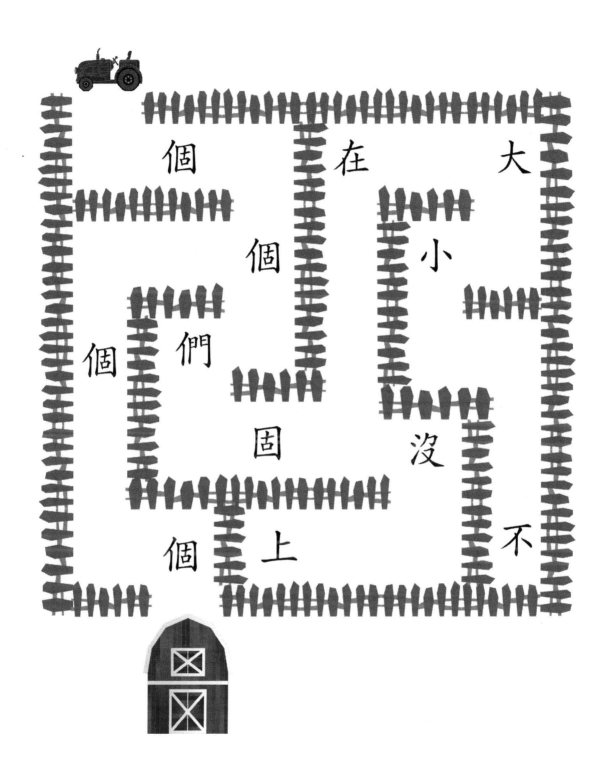

請將有「個」字的地方著色。

Color the areas with the character 個.

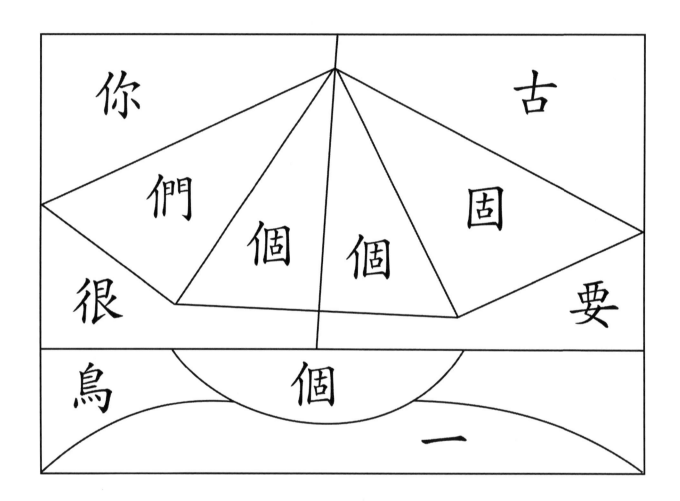

唸唸看
Read-Aloud

- 我家有一個爸爸。
  There is a dad in my family.

- 我家有一個媽媽。
  There is a mom in my family.

- 我的個頭很大。
  My height is very tall.

- 我家沒有小鳥。
  There are no little birds in my home.

- 我頭上有花。
  There is a flower on my head.

恭喜你完成了這一課，請回到第三頁將本課的星星塗上顏色。

Congratulations! You have completed a lesson. Please color the star for this lesson on page 3.

獎狀

Certificate of Achievement

恭喜

Congratulations to

完成漢字遊戲第一冊。
特發此狀以資鼓勵！

for completing Early Start Chinese Workbook 1.

日期 Date

簽名 Signature

Made in the USA
Las Vegas, NV
13 January 2021